WHERE I LIVE

Written By
E.C. Andrews

Letters from Around the World

KidHaven PUBLISHING

Published in 2025 by
KidHaven Publishing, an Imprint of
Greenhaven Publishing, LLC
2544 Clinton St., Buffalo, NY 14224

Written by: E.C. Andrews
Edited by: Elise Carraway
Designed by: Amelia Harris

All facts, statistics, web addresses and URLs in this book were verified as valid and accurate at time of writing. No responsibility for any changes to external websites or references can be accepted by either the author or publisher.

Cataloging-in-Publication Data

Names: Andrews, E.C.
Title: Where I live / E.C. Andrews.
Description: Buffalo, New York : KidHaven Publishing, 2025. | Series: Letters from around the world | Includes glossary and index.
Identifiers: ISBN 9781534546899 (pbk.) | ISBN 9781534546905 (library bound) | ISBN 9781534546912 (ebook)
Subjects: LCSH: Dwellings--Juvenile literature. | Home--Juvenile literature.
Classification: LCC GT172.A534 2025 | DDC 392.3'6--dc23

Manufactured in the United States of America

CPSIA compliance information: Batch #CSKH25
For further information contact Greenhaven Publishing LLC at 1-844-317-7404.

Please visit our website, www.greenhavenpublishing.com.
For a free color catalog of all our high-quality books, call toll free 1-844-317-7404 or fax 1-844-317-7405.

Find us on

Image Credits

All images are courtesy of Shutterstock.com, unless otherwise specified. With thanks to Getty Images, Thinkstock Photo, and iStockphoto. Cover images – NataLT, Akane1988, estherpoon, Fourleaflover, Puwadol Jaturawutthichai, Tartila, cheerywave, The img, In Green, Gus And. Recurring images – KanKhem, Olga_C. 2 – Mari Dambi, meandart, ina9. 4–5 – Drazen Zigic, Murvin. 6–7 – f11photo, CrackerClips Stock Media, danceyourlife, Gus And, Ysami, Neliakott. 8–9 – R.M. Nunes, urosr, Henk Bogaard, Slowga, Illerlok_xolms. 10–11 – Nomad1988, StockImageFactory.com, Lailul Murroh, meandart. 12–13 – Alias Studiot Oy, Sensvector, kelttt, Timo Newton-Syms from Chalfont St Giles, Bucks, UK, CC BY-SA 2.0, via Wikimedia Commons. 14–15 – f11photo, JEONGHYEON NOH, cheerywave, Giuseppe_R, Yaoinlove. 16–17 – fizkes, AlinArt, Ragoon, Immanuel Giel 13:35, 4 June 2007 (UTC), Public domain, via Wikimedia Commons. 18–19 – world of vector, Malikov Aleksandr, In Green. 20–21 – oneinchpunch, Nana Rosdiana, crapwood15, The img. 22–23 – Sunny studio, Mari Dambi, fizkes, johavel, The img.

CONTENTS

Words that look like <u>this</u> can be found in the glossary on page 24.

LETTERS FROM EVERYWHERE

Hi! I am Ben. I live in the U.S. I love writing letters to my pen pals from around the world. We tell each other what life is like in our countries.

I told my pen pals about the Sunday dinners we have every weekend at my home. We spend time with family who don't live with us. Gram and Grandpa drive a long way to join us.

A LETTER FROM ITALY

Hello! I am Francesca. My family is from Italy. We just moved into a new house in the Italian city of Venice. In Venice, we travel by boat instead of driving or using a bus.

The water bus in Venice is called a vaporetto.

Panettone is my favorite kind of bread! What is yours?

Our friends and family came over and gave us some panettone. Panettone is an Italian sweet bread. Bread is sometimes given to new homeowners as a wish that they will never go hungry.

A LETTER FROM NAMIBIA

I am Uatika. I am from Namibia in Africa. My family and I are part of the Himba <u>tribe</u>. The Himba are seminomadic. This means we move around a lot but always go back to our village.

It is very hot and dry here. Some of us cover our skin and hair in otjize to protect us from the sun. Otjize is a mixture of fat and red ochre, which comes from clay.

I love the way otjize feels and smells.

A LETTER FROM INDIA

Hello. I am Rani. My family and I live in India. We do not wear any kind of outdoor footwear in our house. This is our way of showing respect. It also helps keep the house clean.

I live with my parents, two sisters, my grandpa, and my cousins. A lot of my friends also live with their older relatives. We all help each other around the house. We are very close.

How many people live in your home?

A LETTER FROM FINLAND

My name is Henrik. My family and I live in Finland. We have our own sauna by our home. A sauna is a type of hot room that we sit in. It is very relaxing.

This is what our sauna looks like!

Our sauna is a traditional Finnish smoke sauna. It is heated by burning wood. In Finland, lots of people have a sauna at their home. All my friends have one!

This is the inside of a sauna.

A LETTER FROM SOUTH KOREA

My name is Mi-Cha and I live in South Korea. Tomorrow, my little brother will turn one year old! First birthdays are very important here. My family does a special ceremony called doljabi.

We will lay out things such as flowers, books, and teapots for my little brother to go and touch. Whatever he touches first is said to be a clue about what his future job will be.

I think he will touch the flowers and be a gardener!

A LETTER FROM GERMANY

Hello! My name is Gerta and my family is from Germany. My sister is getting married this weekend. In Germany, we do something called Polterabend just before family members get married.

My sister and me

Polterabend is when we go to the bride's home and smash lots of dishes and plates. The bride and her future husband clean it up. This tradition shows how they will always work together in the future.

A LETTER FROM GREECE

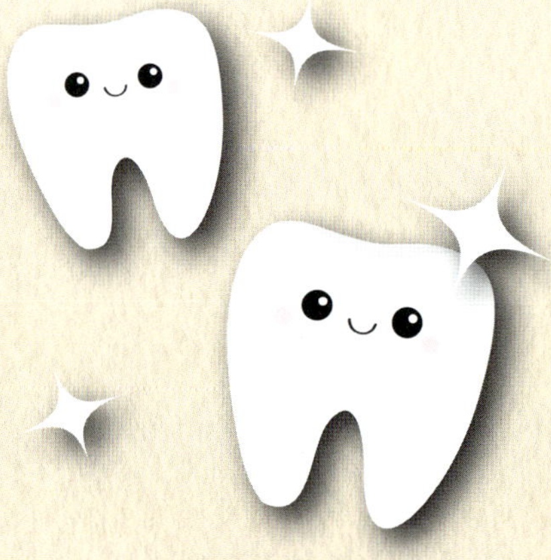

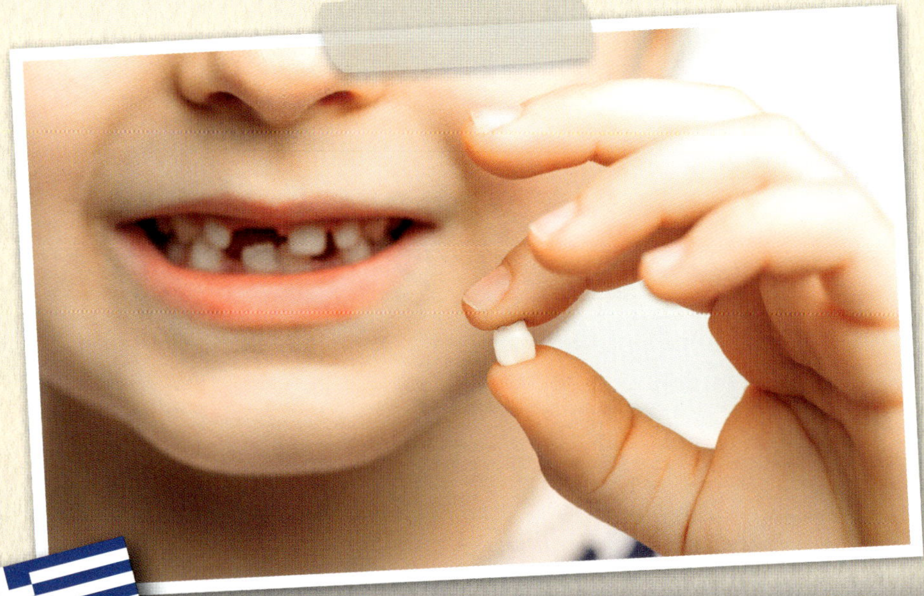

My name is Christos. My home is in Greece. Today, one of my baby teeth fell out. In Greece, we throw our baby teeth onto the roof of the home we grow up in.

We have to throw our teeth as straight as possible. This is said to bring good luck and help us grow our brand-new adult teeth.

A LETTER FROM THE UAE

My name is Amir. My home is in the United Arab Emirates (UAE). It is very important that guests feel welcome in our home. We practice something called karam, which is a way of treating guests.

Karam is another word for generosity.

We always serve our guests tea and coffee. We prepare lots of foods for our guests to choose from. It is important that the food and drink does not run out!

EVERYWHERE IS DIFFERENT

People's homes are different all around the world. My pen pals all have their own family traditions. This is part of their <u>culture</u>. It is so exciting to learn about how other children live!

What is life like in your culture? Do you have any special traditions in your home? You should write to me about it. I would love to be your pen pal!

GLOSSARY

ceremony	a formal occasion celebrating achievements, people, or religious events
culture	the traditions, ideas, and ways of life of a group of people
generosity	showing kindness towards others
relatives	members of the same family
respect	feeling that something or someone is important
traditional	to do with something that has been done for a long time
tribe	a group of people who have their own traditions and culture that is often made up of closely linked family groups

INDEX